What's Inside?

by Mary Jane Martin

SCHOLASTIC INC.

New York   Toronto   London   Auckland   Sydney

Copyright © 1994 by Scholastic Inc.
All rights reserved. Published by Scholastic Inc.
Printed in the U.S.A.
ISBN 0-590-27361-2
ISBN 0-590-29204-8 (meets NASTA specifications)

2 3 4 5 6 7 8 9 10   09   01 00 99 98 97 96 95 94

What's inside?

It's a baby chicken.
That's what's inside.

What's inside?

It's a baby turtle.
That's what's inside.

What's inside?

It's a baby penguin.
That's what's inside.

What's inside?

It's a baby fish.
That's what's inside.

What's inside?

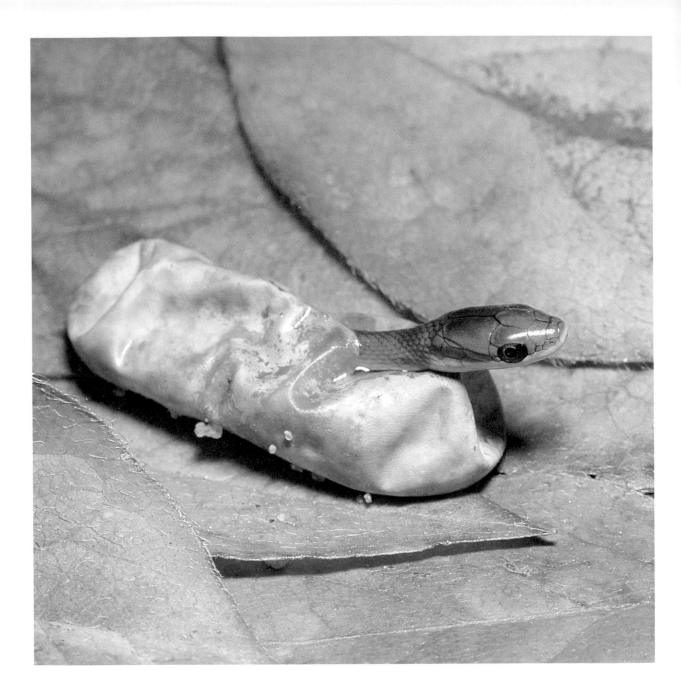

It's a baby snake.
That's what's inside.

What's inside?

It's a baby heron.
That's what's inside.

What's inside?

They're baby salamanders.
Aren't they amazing?